FIELD

MUSIC

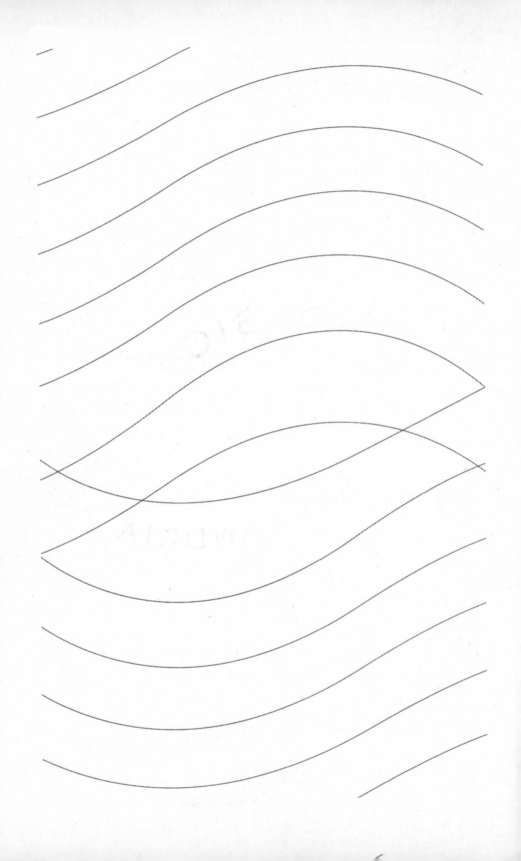

FIELD MUSIC

POEMS

ALEXANDRIA HALL

ecco

An Imprint of HarperCollins*Publishers*

HarperCollins books may be purchased for educational, business, or sales promotional use. For information, please email the Special Markets Department at SPsales@harpercollins.com.

Ecco® and HarperCollins® are trademarks of HarperCollins Publishers.

FIRST EDITION

Designed by Michelle Crowe

Library of Congress Cataloging-in-Publication Data has been applied for.

ISBN 978-0-06-300838-0

20 21 22 23 24 LSC 10 9 8 7 6 5 4 3 2 1

For my parents

CONTENTS

FIELD MUSIC

COWBIRD

All of this damage is already done:
the meadows inflamed and gone blonde
    with rash goldenrod. Nothing ever stays
where it ought: runoff dragged into the river
by summer rains from shit-covered fields—
    my thickly perfumed Vermont. The morning

glories creep up the shafts of the garden
vegetables, their seductive curls choking
    out my small plot. Sometimes we can't see
the dangers we feed, that we nurture,
like the warbler who cares for the cowbird
    planted in her nest, a deep and doubling

hunger fed as the nestlings starve
in their crowded bowl. I know
    I'm not invited. I want
to love something. Not to open my mouth
like the long, smooth flower
    of a ravenous weed.

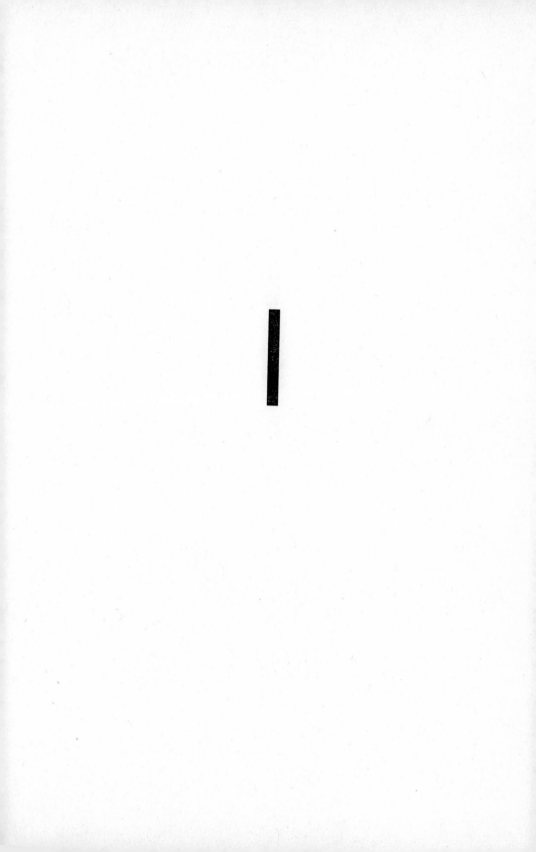

TRAVEL NARRATIVE

There was too much moon over the night in Middlebury
so I put a man's face in front of it, and then I loved
that man. There was too much hair soaked in sweat
along the trails in Galicia, so I cut off my head

and put a man's face in front of it, and then my love
poured out like water over a copper bust, or the rain
along the trails in Galicia, where I cut off my head
and kept walking. There were too many monuments

pouring water over their copper busts, a verdigris rain
on the fountain of the Hamburger Rathaus. Too much to remember
so I kept walking, learning the names of too many monuments.
I wanted to go home. I do remember

the Hygieia fountain at the Hamburger Rathaus. Remember
there were too many shadows and they changed too often.
Remember I wanted to go home,
which was a shadow, so I didn't.

ON BEAUTY

He run out of propane and the cold licked the trailer like a dog with a hurt paw. *Pa*, my brother would have called him, if I'd had a brother, if I'd a been him, had he been at all.

All night the whimpering hills. Transmission on the truck's broke. Winter pushes my father and his home and his froze-up pipes and piles of scrap to a grater and grates. These gift-basket ideas solve little. *Awful nice a ya*, wheezes Pa. Sometimes my brother speaks through me.

How's the new beau, he coughs. He took me to the city, I says, and we went to the Met and I loved the Picassos and Degas and when he watched me stumble over a Cézanne, he says it's *challenging*. So I stood there all night trying to meet that messy landscape's glance, massaging its junk, snapping its bra, growling lowly in its ear, baring my teeth.

I will not back down from the challenge of "the Beautiful," but like my brother, I study it as a battlefield. Learn its ins and outs until I feel it, real as the rough, brown wool of my grandmother's crochet owl that still hangs on my father's wall amidst the howling, where winter is a tunnel and what's beautiful is as easy as spotting the light. Spotting the deer in the field.

FIELD MUSIC

Wringing out the wind chimes, the night leaves
a hole for a spotlight and my hands callous
over the goats' singing. Somebody killed
my cat, not in the way Dad made the sheep

click. You know, I've got half a mind to halve
you, hot as a Salamander, foul as a skidsteer.
I ain't chicken. I saw Cat Ballou, the horse
that fell through the ceiling. She was unbridled.

I hope when I grow up, I marry a boy I know
so we both know what to listen for: the sound
of falling tips the stirrup in the ear. Mom says *ancient*
like *ank-shint* and every time I hear *eggshells*

or *ankle-shins*. I stay up at night, the goats
bleating in the barn, the barn bleeding
into the goats, wind-jiggled, like Dad's trailer
where I sit alone, waiting for the cockcrow to blear

the fields. In the parking lot of the deli, pulling onions
off a sub, my mother shrieks, *Crimus ditch*, but I hear
the four-wheeler's back tires, two weeks ago, tearing
up the mud pit, thrown back like a spooked horse.

Dad says he can sing like a Kawasaki. He says
he's got some good *idears*. I know how to shoot
a gun. The .22 kicked my weak shoulder but I lied
and said it was fun, just like I lied at my first confession,

scared the priest would ask me to think harder or speak
up. I never talk down. I never say *shit*. The gravel
nibbles my toes. I know about sex. It's not a cardinal
flying into the wrong window. The neighbor's

puppies vacuum the gravel from the bitch.
I don't like to call her that, but Jimmy does. We dig
a hole under the uprooted hickory and wiggle
our split ears into the culvert. The line of trees

laid down after the ice storm slicked them. Dad hit
Grandpa till the state troopers strobed
the kitchen, staining my sweater. Grandma says
creek like *crick* and I wait for the violins.

If you keep kicking somebody, music
will come out eventually.

SYRINX

We don't play songs here; we touch
them. Like elephants mulling
over the dead, music is a handling.
Listen to the sounds
of a touched thing: a body, the panpipe,
the waste garnishing the roads
that lead out of Cusco. *Tocar* is creation.

On the bus, two young boys sing
"Ojos Azules" like a couple of tanagers
that trill and stir the passengers.
I felt something once. A broken reed
licked my foot on the slick banks.

Ojos azules no llores. Take and cut
my soft frame into parts, arrange
by size, bind by catgut. *No llores
ni te enamores*. I never sing
as a thrush in a natural spasm,
but as a ghost of that fit.
As a long sigh that brushes
the bones. A whisper rolled
through the stalks. *Llorarás
cuando me vaya*. To be touched,
    ultimately, by a sickle—
    cuando remedio ya no haya—
    and feel only the wind.

MY LOVE

Turn a latex glove inside out—
    that's what it looks like.
        Every part of me aches
its belligerence in your direction.
        Did I wake you. Show me your teeth.

My love swims you, your shoulders
    like hard sails under the green curls.
        Doesn't sink. Doesn't stink at all.
Small powder around the moon.
        No, an eggshell. I was baking. Slight odor.

Call it a fragrance. I fall it sometimes,
    sleeping. Didn't laugh that way.
        Why are you angry. Something hurts very badly.
Look I'm bleeding it. Hold your body up against mine.
        I'm a pool noodle with too many feelings.

Look good in that dress though.
    That thing that happened once happened again.
        In a kitchen in Brooklyn.
At a rooftop screening. Under the table in Middlebury.
        Happened to me differently. It depended me to you.

I'm off the deep end, but I'm buoyant.
      Your hard plastic body cuts the waves.
          You are my mean hero. Give me some too.
Dance silly for me, honey. Baby. My love. I fall it sometimes
         but I laugh well, walking backward out of myself.

GEOSMIN

Her shoulders were much smaller
than mine. I wasn't sure

how to touch them. If a man
ever felt this way about my body,

how could he
go on touching me?

It was surely a very bad thing.
The wet earth

smelled richer then,
in Vermont, when it let the rain

all the way in, let itself
be soaked through.

SMOKE

At Paynes Prairie, before the fire,
an armadillo's remains catch the light
like a Spanish coronet.
I put too much stock in the cicadas

who hum along to my appliances,
who *relevé* in time with my refrigerator.
I, too, can swan dive out of myself,
but then what? The boys say

there's a moment in spring
when the lindens smell like cum.
I try to imagine the blossoms erupting,
abashed, staining the throw.

Soon the thick smoke will grip
the interstate and we will only hear
the guard rail, the tires,
the little broken carapace.

THE FIRST TIME

It was boring—in a field
under the stars, wrapped
in sleeping bags he'd taken
from his parents' house.
Nearby the vague silhouette
of a farm tractor, wind slipping
through the rust spots of the drowsy
pickup, and the thick cricket music.
Every so often, the soft interference
of a pair of far off headlights gliding
North in silence along the highway.

Nice guy, sure. Romantic, I guess.
I didn't want romantic. I wanted
him to suck my lips off my face,
spit them out, change shape, turn
ugly, wanted him to toss his head
back and never roll it up,
evaporating like a tired dandelion.

Amid the stirring of field mice
and garter snakes, I longed for
the jolt of a hand caught in the thresher.
I wanted the night like a spider
to lift one arm after another
and climb into me while he washed
out into the long, wet sky, which was blue.

THE BODY AT NIGHT

I dropped out of my body in long clean streams
like water through a colander, easily and ordinarily.

Most nights my body was consigned to a pull-out couch
next to the body of my bully. I was not afraid of the dark

but of what was discernible. The facts were present
like an unpleasant smell. Every morning sulfur

from the paper plant advanced over the lake and lingered
unremarkably. There was nothing extraordinary

about the snow globes on the dresser, the knots
that looked like eyes in the wood paneling,

my face pressed to the asphalt, spit and blood
on my cheek, her body at night so close to mine.

But while she slept, I think now, looking back, my body
inflated, got so big it filled the room, the whole house

even, like caulk, like cement, covering everything.

I CONTAIN MYSELF NEEDFULLY

Of all the things at Mary's house, I recall the look of the larkspur overcome by the lavender.

Sure, I see the rapture of Bernini's Saint Teresa, though the stone looks so cold.

You have to be able to leave yourself before you can truly leave another.

Last night I danced until I could have been slipped out of.

But there's that *I* again, that *that I again*.

Morning is a despot. I comply with each humiliating demand.

Before the renovation, birds flew down the chimney. My mother shrieked when they pierced the living room.

This move is called the inflatable man. I call this one the trash compactor.

How long is the average feeling of remorse? Rough estimate.

J says, *There is no unseeing, no undoing*. But I put it all in words until it withdraws completely.

My neighbor who kept pigeons in a coop on the roof lost all five hundred in the fire. A drone video shows the view from above. No sound. Just the building heaving light.

SOMETHING IMPORTANT PUT CLUMSILY AWAY

He covered the expenses. Held the small of my back.
They gave me ginger ale and crackers. I didn't say

I felt woozy. Whimpering and dry heaving
on the bathroom floor, I called his name and he came.

Dragged myself up. I never liked his mother
because she never liked me. Afraid of the damage

when the damage leans over. I never liked his mother
but that night I saw a picture of her in a white sweater,

young and pregnant with his older brother.
I started wearing a white sweater. We didn't tell

our mothers. He had an old car that kept breaking down
and he left it running while he filled the tank. It scared me.

He would drive me anywhere. When my body was a cup
tipped over. Then I hated him. When he reached

for the small under my sweater, I shrieked, *go, get out*
you monster you dull slop you infinite problem.

Can't fit the holes back in. They keep leaking through the cracks.

ON LOOKING

I began like her, alone and thinking, wrapped
in blue before a dark ledge, chin cocked
and looking slant. In the other room,

M was occupied with the Cézannes.
His eyes moved into and across the paints.
I didn't leave the young woman, her pink

and dreamed-over city, her sheer,
bright ibises implanted there and listening.
These are the birds

I've been trying to speak to
from this space of waiting
for the painter's restless hand.

WALKING IN REVERSE

Arrival steeped in a long sleep. From the side
it looked like river water. Home receded,
returning in small questions. Inside were words
like *nightshade*. Back there. Smell of the granary

in winter. Here there's a church in the city center
and the birds with their own bells scream back.
It has a nice ring to it. I try to imitate but it sounds
like: *I've got a lot of praise for someone if you'll just*

let me. A tired guest in other people's houses.
Rules you can take or leave, but not give
or stay. You shouldn't spoil dinner or dinner
conversation. You should call home. Home

is where the mail goes. The lake was different
after the mist rose. After the mist left the groceries
at the store. Yes, we've met before. No, it's fine, really.
My cold hands, my chaise longue. For whom will I heat

up the leftovers. Hi, sweetie. Poor baby. My mother,
the speedboat. I would write but I haven't. To my
honey-dripping basketball, my love in the round,
my anger, my anchor, my shape ever in relief.

IN THE NETS

On the coast I saw nets, and lacking
a good sense of boundaries, I saw
myself, made mostly of holes, myself,
a boundary for the washed-through,
the held. Could this not be about capture?

After lunch the man I loved told his mother
all the ways she'd failed him. I tried to stick
to my business of the slipped-by and the built-up,
tried to disappear from the table, fiddled
with a salt-stung cut, watched the beach

where a row of baby girls like new birds
were planted with their toes outstretched
to feel the water rush and recede, the young father
clowning around them dizzily. I've been failed,
too. It pours out at inopportune moments.

I pitied the timid beach dog, her cracked
and sandy teats. I want to be full
with the way things move through me.
I want to be a mother again, porous, stretched
in place by the floats and weights.

FILLING STATION

after Elizabeth Bishop

Oh, but it is dirty!
We lean over the Gulf
pumps, filling with fumes,
filling the tanks. What a luxury
to fill.

~

Never my legs, never my hands,
never my hair. The vulgarity
of the begonia or the leggy girl
with her plaid barrette. Never
the thick knuckles of the gearheads,
never, not once, to be extraneous
as lipstick, to be beautiful.

~

At night, the older boys in trucks
chuckle and rattle and spit dip.

Look, I found elegance
in a grease pit.

~

Filling our bras, our mouths,
our slender hands.

Say it.
They're dirty.

~

To fill, to soak,
to brim, but never spill.

~

And yet, to fill one thing
implies an emptying.

~

Out of the greasy radio slips
"Never My Love." Never the hand
that turned it on. Only the notion
that that hand, that oily hand,
would do it—when it seems meant
only to fill

~

And fill and fill
unlike that highfalutin chiseled
giggle. A giddy snort.
An *Oh, so adorable, the poor,*
and their deplorable décor!

~

Filling our beds, our bellies,
our backseats. Filling even this—
who'd believe it? Look,
somebody loves us all.

THE LAKE HOUSE

Ferrisburgh keeps nothing but the smell of skunk and lilacs
        and the two lines of the headlights swimming
over the dirt road like sturgeon under the water.
        I tried to dive in once, up on Satterly Road
where I wrecked the Chevy, threw it over
        like a breaching whale in a swell of broken glass,
then landed belly-up in the ditch, dirt holding
        the tire marks like a child holding her breath.
Smells like skunk tonight, doesn't it? And lilacs.

At night, when the neighbors' cows get loose and sashay
        around the yard, this trailer's just a dinghy slapped
in their waves. Once the lilacs dragged me down
        that narrow dirt road to a lake house, the scent
like thousands of purple fingers pulling
        and waving, always moving. But skunk smell—
the animal either dead or scared—just hangs there,
        still. Pummeled by high beams and tires, it stays.
At the lake house I was strange, surrounded

by nice things, trying on fancy clothes or posing
      nude before the grand bay windows. Things don't unrot
just become more rotten. Those windows made the lake
      between the hills into a mouth, opened wide to swallow
them. To swallow the lilac, too. Sometimes I get so small,
      but the sound I make is as big as a shrew caught
in a mouse trap, thrashing around the cupboard
      like frantic knocking at the door. No one ever knocks
at the door. Occasionally, though, the cows float by.

TOUCH COMES THROUGH ME

like dirty water through a drain.
Night sweat on the back of winter.
I might hold myself like that,

too tightly. I can feel the weight
of my hand resting on my leg
but not the pulp of my thigh

at my fingertip. There are, I'm told,
two sides to touch. On the porch
in late spring I heard touch rip open,

loud as canvas. In summer, touch
ate through me like a tapeworm,
taking me up under each supermoon.

If I were a system of pipes, I swear,
I'd never burst. I could love with a velvet
mouth. When touch leaves nothing

terrible happens. I am still. I fill
like a bag of leaves at the edge
of the lawn. Look at it now, so clear.

BLOOM

My daughter lost her head in a moon accident,
at night, in these arms. I cratered her and sang
without a love of my own love of my own love
of my own love. I meant to be full, not fall.
I dropped myself in the kitchen. It was as if
she could hear me. Her ears opened outward
but the holes were inside her. I held her
like a bunch of still birds, like a potted palm.
Light moved across and away from her.
When the glasses broke, a moon
took the breath that cut my bird in the dark.

CHACALA

Some nets lie on the ocean floor, unattended.

He had so much skin, warm and waiting to be handled.

Even the lizards skimmed their fleshy bellies on the ceiling.

When you catch something, does it thrash inside you?

At night while the cuijas made a kissing sound,
he showed me how he'd rather be touched.

I felt the part inside me that's made of holes, that generates no heat.

Do you let the animal pull its shape into you?

Do you let yourself fall on its form?

DIRT SONG

The berries are in season. The sea
knocks into the low rocks
but will not seep
into the dirt of my body.

Shame, it was my nice dress.
I hold him like a hot coal
in the cool hollow I've dug.
I soak and rinse for him,

stain the linens, come
unpacked at the table,
make a scene when I spill
the dirt of my body.

I left home like a tick
leaves the tall grass,
but guilt is soft. I sink
into it like a tree into rot.

His warm fingers rake
the dirt of my body.

SONNET WITH A LINE FROM WORDSWORTH

This ushered in through a yawn a divide
and to be numbed or to be deadened.

Blistered and in that dawn the bees aligned.
What the bees sang was barely leavened.

Spilled water on the divan and jived,
the far-flung berries reckoned.

Brisk washing if the pond should be the hive,
but with the tongue, cut every weapon.

It's busted on the lawn. The bees alight,
but haven't stung. A wary procession.

Bliss was it in that dawn to be alive,
But to be young was very heaven!

This wasted private song couldn't deprive
the ruby lung its buried venom.

FISHING

Dad took me fishing after school. He brought Pringles and soda.
All the bait shops had signs out front that read *Nightcrawlers*. They
came in a Styrofoam dish from the fridge. Inside it they were naked
and dirty. I didn't want to bait the hook so he did it for me. It must
have been like a prick in a soft grape, a thumbtack through a baby's
finger. Then they were pierced and living. We sat for a long time at
the edge of the footbridge. The water was still and reedy. Dad caught
a few little ones and he threw them back. They were wet and slick
and wriggling. When I felt a snag, I reeled it in. A brush in a line
through the reeds. Out of the water I lifted an already dead thing,
pale white with an old hook and line sprouting out of the gills. At
the end of the string hung a horrible ornament. No gasping, no
writhing, just the sagging weight.

AFTER HEARING OF MY FATHER'S ILLNESS

I went to the state fair.
From the Ferris wheel, I could see
the dust from the demo derby
settling over the stadium,
reminding me of him
in the early mornings,
going out to feed the goats
whose bleats, he said, sounded
like his name, *Mark*, held out
in tremolo. I strolled down
the midway with a candy apple
and watched the animals
in the farm tents, swarmed
by kids with sticky hands.
I played the water
gun game and won.
When I was young,
my father was invincible,
at the shooting range or driving
trucks through the mud, ripping
up Ethier's fields.

On my way out, I stopped to watch
the mechanical bull as it spilled
one man all over the mats
like a pitcher of water jerked
upward—some to the left,

a bit behind, a few drops drizzling
down the right. In a matter of seconds
he'd splashed everywhere
and was mopped up, shaking
his head, smiling as he walked
out down the midway. The next rider
mounted its broad back and nodded.
The operator spoke like a metronome
evenly into a microphone: *one.*
The rider's first fall, immediate.
Get back on the bull. The man obeyed
the operator's low, portato voice.
One, hold onto it.
two, stay on the bull. three.
The ride started slowly.
A forward dip, then the rearing
up. Always alongside it,
the operator's voice warm
and distant, like a French horn,
counting: *four, hold on. five.*
The rider's body sagged
down one side of the machine,
one leg still slung over the back, *stay*
on the bull. His shoulder finally sank
to the padded mat.
Get back on
the bull. Get
back on the
bull. Get back
on the bull.

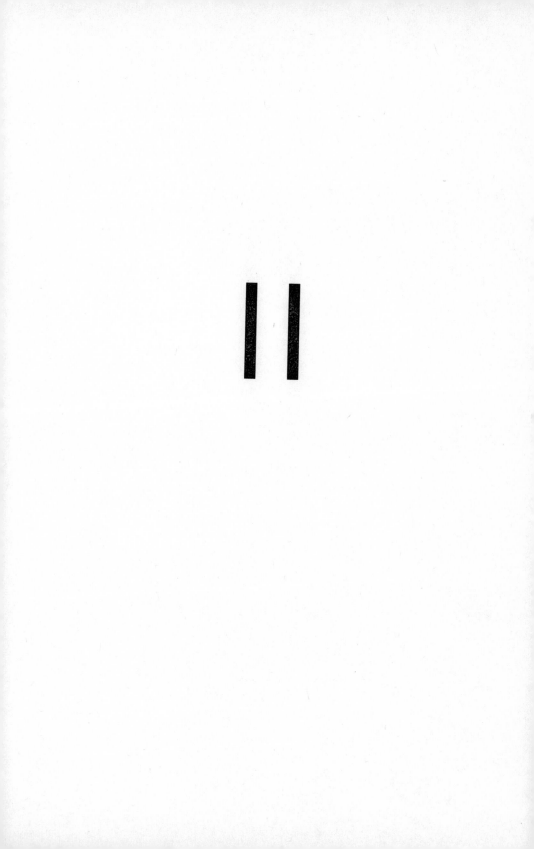

HAVING BEEN

Pile of stones in the dawn mist of Biduedo.
Orange rind thrown from the back of a pickup.

Papa's hand over his lost sternum. The potted ivy.
Name of the stillborn son. Scarce glimpse

of wild turkeys before the line of trees. Bird's nest
in the chimney. Wasps in the attic. Chipped blue

paint on the fishing boat in Portree. A couple
of empties wedged into the sand at Revere

Beach. Stray dogs dodging cars at the Oxxo.
Water level marked on the bluffs. The peonies

glutted and collapsed on the driveway in June.
I am undone, not by grief, but abundance.

ON ART

Art is nice. It is very, very nice. In her lifetime, my grandmother painted dozens of pictures—copies of scenic postcards or images of yawning puppies in boots. These boots are made for walking. These shit-kickers. Oh, these? Just a little old something I had lying around.

My grandmother was a little old something, too. She had a scary scarcely. Lips opened like a chicken with a broken beak when she sold her pictures to the folks at the Country Kitchen diner. Why oh why. Was it art for Pete's sake?

Art is pretty. It is only just or it is almost not. Because it is old like my grandmother and valiant like these boots it has a must. I mean it is an odor and an ought. It has a little pink tongue.

What's the difference between a big blunder and a little diddle? I did a very bad thing. Verily I say underwear.

Poetry is unsafe. I commit this violence to shape it with words. If I say it wrong, it might be better. I apologize for all my gross ejaculations. Shame. Shame, shame.

Rilke says to a young poet that things aren't so sayable.   happens where words haven't. It is very virginal. *Betreten* meaning to enter. *Betreten* meaning embarrassed. Abashedly I push these words into. Words like marshmallows, words like clogged pores. O my mom, I am heartily sorry for having this tendency.

I would like to show you something other than this sick deformity. Unfortunately you'll have to look under this cover, here. Stick your head in the casket. Fine, just put your hand out. It was a terrible thing to do. O, my head, I am heartily sorry. O, my heart, my achy, breaky heart.

Art is beautiful. What is beautiful is true. When the imagination seizes it, you should never put a spoon in its mouth. It is nice to be stirred, but alarming to be shaken. You shook me all night long. I said shake, rattle, and roll. This is a test of the emergency broadcast system. This is a false alarm. This is a downright lie.

HOME

Why a man's sink always has a smell.
Why you told her her cheeks jiggle

when she walks. Why not to touch a baby
bird. How the plow drags the snow.

Who answers the door. If the window's painted
shut. When you're being ugly. Where to meet

if separated. If your feet are wet. Why the stain
won't come out. What it looks like

in the bathroom mirror. When the smoke
filled the dining room. Where it hurts.

If you did your best but. How it sounds
when it's touched. When they burned the nest.

A SERIES OF LOSSES

We rented the trailer on the goat farm. Dad worked there
under the table. I didn't know what that meant, but he said,

if Mom starts to pry just say I'm helping out. The farmer
was an older lady and Dad said she wasn't well.

I used to hear it as, making ends *meat*, and I'd see a roast
at the edge of everything. I love someone and I visit him

in Baltimore. His apartment is as cold as the farm
was, once it all started dying and being left around.

Your accent comes out when you say what *like that.*
I'm soft to him, like a child, when he teases me.

I am a soft but reckless creature. Lives, whole and partial,
have been left around. My father, now a crescent somewhere.

I am ready to be devastated and I practice nightly,
my head on this chest, soaking his T-shirt, bawling

like the goats did, in Cornwall,
above the black fields.

DESIRE

As when learning a new language,
I feel the separateness of my body:
the mouth trying to form

the right shape to sound
the difference between *Hölle*
and *Höhle*—one hell, one

hole—the mouth itself
a pit, a void contorted,
through which we voice,

fumble over vowels. The palate
learning a posture, the mouth
given a mouth, given a cup

to be filled, to be poured,
given a breath blown through
a scrap of lace. The mouth

like the moon curling
into a small crater—*Mond*
or *Mund*—the vowels

confused again, the tongue
quivering naked in the gorge.
I want you, a pang.

Press your hand
like a roll of gauze
to the wound.

SLUMBER PARTY

The string of lights by the shade gives
two silhouettes away: two bodies,
or the bodies are two shadow puppets
at a junior high school slumber party.
When the girls snap their fingers,
the shadows are dancing. When they clap,
it means they're fighting. When they pull

back my hair and say I'd make the prettiest boy,
I feel pride like the meat of a peach with a cold pit.
One girl points down the night at Hospital Creek
where the ghosts are. One girl knows how to walk
in heels. I know the American Goldfinch
has a contact call birders liken to singing
po-ta-to-chip. I'm here, where are you? I've become

pretty well acquainted with the firmness of a grip,
at least how I imagine it from the image on the blinds.
When the two shadows touch, a clinking sound.
When one girl steps away, all the other girls hide
and, returning, I'm as soft as a dropped apple rolled
into the center of the empty room. Test one, two.
Testing one, two. Are you there? *Potato chip?*

They're twisted up laughing. I don't laugh. I watch
one last shadow: this one looks like a tree being felled.
When the girls shake with laughter, a rainy breeze
slaps through the leaves. When they sleep, the tree
is chopped down into firewood. When they leave
in the morning, branches scrape the window,
two pale fingers part the blinds.

PRACTICE TEST FOR INSATIABLE LONELINESS

1. Absence
a) makes the heart grow in vines up the latticework.
b) makes dinner and leaves the dishes.
c) makes change like the man at the laundromat,
   carefully on the wooden counter.
d) makes love cruelly.

2. Which of the following does *not* apply
a) My hunger is an ugly baby that needs touch.
b) My hunger has a very big mouth.
c) If you leave your name and number
   my hunger will get back to you as soon as possible.
d) No hunger here.

3. To improve mood: practice gratitude.
I, for one, am grateful for the following beds
I do not have to make:
river bed,
nail bed,
truck bed,
hotbed of deceit and suspicion.

4. True or False: Good grief.

5. My ardor is greater than/less than/equal to a barn fire.

6. Untouched, the fire keeps burning.
Most wounds heal without asking.
In two to three sentences, explain
the bright gash of my barn on the night.

7. True or False: If my hunger is mechanical
then my vacuum bag is a sad sack.

8. Draw a diagram of not looking. Plot
points A and B where lines come close
but do not intersect.

9. One man's trash
a) is out of the office, returning Tuesday.
b) contains multitudes.
c) would like to thank you
   for your generous donation.
d) is eventually revealed to be just trash.

ON MUSIC

By the pool the vultures
circled and perched on the roof
to watch his naked body rock

over mine. Danger
is never as interesting
as the possibility

of danger. As if wanting
me were a song he hummed
without knowing, I listened

with eyes closed and waited
for the pattern to break.
The chachalaca sang

like scrap metal dragged
across more scrap metal.
We lay all day like fruit

burst open for the birds to take
and awoke at night to a crashing
outside our room,

which was not a break-in
but the crude drum
of the mangos falling

in the garden
out of their ripe skins.
No pomp, just bruising.

ON ART

Even the softest things, under the right conditions become sharp. Cold hardens skin, nipples; makes distinct the supple scents of laundry detergent and cigarette smoke. The cold let all the air out of the words and now our trip is delayed. A room full of new, squishy babies so cute I could just squeeze them, oh, I could just eat them up. So a love becomes annihilation. So we're born into a long, long mouth. So long as there's a form, there's an edge.

The sublime according to Burke is terrible. The sublime according to Kant, boundless. When we aimed at imagining God we didn't have to try so hard to say it wrong. Now that we know, the seams are showing: precisely at the petals like panty lines. If we keep blowing all the stones to pieces, all the old will fold like new over itself, it seems to me, if you just squeeze and squeeze and squeeze.

DEALING WITH THE ABSENCE

In winter the flats froze over
and made for decent skating.
Glazed hard and wet, grooved
with skate scars, pale stalks
of grass standing clear through.

Those fields where the boys
went mudding and burned trash.
I've been a natural thing.
It's not like the sounds
of the boys' bonfires. It's here,

in the kitchen, scraping my insides
like a jar of honey, forgetting
toward the bottom, any need
for measurement. Here at the end,
making it always too sweet.

CONTRITION

                       My gullet is a sham simpering sham
slivering too-tight module. The body of cripes. The body of cripes.
I thought I told you not to. She shook node, node on the flag pole.
I saw some list under musk and tallow. Nothing left of the smut
tunnel, fetid fetish, put stowage, rot tottler, pith pantry. I'm doing
my breast, fuck I'm doing my breadth, no I'm doing my beast, stop
you were the bees. Try harder. I'm waxfully backward between
the *tourterelles*. Hacked be the tarantella. Please don't, in the hintering
brack. Lunar: benign. Be nine, moreover and maladroit. Look
what you've done. Look at your mouth in the sag-patented sunk.
I detest my skins, no my singe, no my sons. Look what you've done.

RELEASE

I'm not sure why I went to her wedding—
I did it for my mother I guess, and to scoff at the trashy

unlit portalets, to watch the dopey groom
take a long step into the bear trap that had once gripped

my ankle. In high school, I found her secret online journal
and didn't show anyone, but I checked back to read

about her mother scolding her through the bathroom door
while she pushed her fingers down her throat and held

her head over the toilet. I always call it getting away,
as in, when I got away from her she set her barbs

into poor Britt, who like a dog with a jaw full of quills,
droop-eyed, could not have predicted the sting

of drawing close to a warm body. I watched
it happen. That's all, just watched. I can't get away

with being angry, with being hot and shrapneled.
I found the hole under the sink where the mouse gets in

and I set the poison out. From the couch in the next room,
I listen as it takes the bright blue pebbles in its mouth.

MY MOTHER THE ASTRONOMER

My mother the astronomer is sick.
They've sifted through the test results and found
nothing. She's seen the charts and diagrams,

the judgment on the doctor's face, when tired,
desperate, she maintains: *In the beginning
there was so much pain.* A drooping planet
rolled over in the night. It was my mother

the astronomer, who dreamed of pushing
a word, a wave, through the thickest layers
of darkness, who cast me like a fragment,
just a rock, before the whole Earth. I rise

and glide into the silent, black water
with my pants rolled to my knees, and I pan
and I pan for her impossible sign.

DREDGE

I didn't know him but I knew the girl who loved him.
It's not my place to put myself at the bottom of the creek.

As hard as I try I can't make anything stop moving.
This twitch. The breeze. The bodies that keep washing away.

If I knew anything about nature, I wouldn't be reading this
guidebook. I would quit pulling when I should be softly rocking.

There is no excuse for the things I've done. People drown
in the gorge every year but we keep coming back to swim.

In the park by the falls, I watched a man eating. Between his legs
his dog waited for a scrap. To feed is to care, not to crave or to carve.

It's not the mouth that starves. If I knew anything about nurture,
I'd know this already. What's the point in stealing

if you have to hide it? I took a lover anyway and let him build up
in my river like a silt deposit. I had a taste for him

without the withdrawal. When he boarded the plane
I had horrible thoughts. As a child it was easy; just touch

the wall and yell *Safety*. I want to know everything
will be alright, which is worry, which is not sorry,

which still says nothing of the boy who went missing
in winter. They had to wait till spring to drag the river.

HUSH

My baby was too heavy to hold.
When I tried to lift her from the car seat
she nearly broke my arms. My baby

was as heavy as a headstone. If she hit
the pavement, she would crack in two.
The migrating birds followed the memorial

lights and flew around homeward
around again homeward around again
deathwardly having lost the moon.

Their falling made a flicker in the lights.
The ground is dirty. You really shouldn't eat
off it. My baby was too heavy to hold

her shape. She rolled into something smaller,
something blunt and featureless,
something dark and sticky in my underwear.

AT DUSK

Shapes pressed into sand by the wind.

The man calling back to you, go under.

His shoulders emerging from the swell.

Bit of green in the sunset.

The water enjoying its mouth, shameless,

swilling the juices of its own warm body.

Wet hair dressing the nape and undressing.

What would he feel inside you?

The waves gradually hardening, turning

under like daylight, as the air farther inland,

without noticing, loosens its grip on the salt.

PROXIMITY

We caught a Helen Frankenthaler show
and ate pistachio ice cream at Sant Ambroeus.
On the train he held me close, reciting
Keats in my ear. From the cab at night,
the city was lengthy and spilling. Lights
from the rooftop. Blood on the bathmat.
This was years ago now. He still holds me

like that on the L so he doesn't have to touch
the railing. On my walk home the trash bags
that line my block jerk and rustle. One thing
still moves another. I am split open anymore.

I like the track at McCarren in the morning
when it's raining and the park is a cold fish gutted
of its runners and walkers, with just a huddle of men
in yellow vests and raincoats collecting litter
near the garbage cans. I like to be alone and moving,

however strained or lopsided, and I like him
to pull my wet face into his chest till I can feel
his breath on my neck, hot and unfresh,
like the gust of air before an oncoming train.

ON TASTE

That night we lay strewn on the grass,
a product of restlessness, like garbage
combed through by skunks who,
though they've had their fill,

keep searching through the scraps
of plastic. I held my fingers out
to find yours. There were mornings
when the rubber tree brushed its hard

leaves against our bedroom window
and shivered. When your hands first
found my vagueness, you traced over
and over the indefinite edges.

We closed our eyes and listened
to the crack of croquet mallets
between the roses and the digitalis.
You want me to tell you about pleasure.

First there was a jolt, a sting, though
it was hard to locate. I squeezed my whole
left hand in my right. It was a hole to slip
through. I still might. I lick

sauce from my knuckles, unwont
to want particularly. Meanwhile, you
are refining your taste in me. You want me
dressed in desire like wet silk.

A desire that looks good on me,
that hugs the detailed curves of fantasy,
instead of this mess, this heaving blur.
Could this be pleasure?

I'll order the same dish I had last night.
I'll have all the gusto of a dead white fish.
I'll order a love that is enough. See
how I unfurl for you like a touched fern,

trembling in damp, green light? It's true
there may be others who'd be full
with me where you are wanting.
The first time you pointed

to the shades of green in the clouds,
I didn't see. It is a pleasure
to be ugly, hungry, and scattered.
It is a pleasure to keep looking.

APPETITE

You can call the chickadees with a repeated psh sound,
like popping tires or an air mattress. My uncle's a birder,

he tells me these things. He can spend hours
behind a pair of binoculars, waiting for the sight

of some rare fistful of feathers. I wish I cared more
about the birds, but I am interested in omens,

which share their roots with ornithology—
the direction of a vulture's flight could help divine

the will of the gods. That, and the willingness of a lamb
to approach the altar. There's a farm in these mountains

run by vegans, who raise Icelandic sheep to feed,
ethically, they say, the appetites of others. Spot

the young rams in the shaking brush. They emerge, as if floating
under thick coats, decked in leaves, weeks before the slaughter.

SPRING CLEANING

In March, fog rinses
out the summit
of Snake Mountain, draining
the remains of The Grand View
after seven minutes
of saturated browns and greens.
One moment, the drizzled vista,
the next, high gray nothing.
Once a hotel, soaked with smoke,
now, clouds shifting
over a slab of foundation.

There's a pile
of empty beetle bodies
between the screen
and the storm window.
When I clean them out
their dust hides
under my fingernails.
Sometimes I wonder
what it's like to be
the one to stumble
upon the dead body
in the woods.

Would the face look
lifelike discarded
in the wet leaves?
In the movies,
to make the sounds
of onscreen fighting,
Foley artists punch slabs
of meat, and sometimes
it feels good. I only touch
myself when I'm angry.

I ought to haul out all
this junk I called winter
and lose it somewhere.
The body loses itself
between slabs of glass
or trail markers.
I like a realistic ending.
Learning is not a smooth insertion
or a brisk switch,
but a slow and painful, then
comforting, then painful rub.
When the lights turned on
they illuminated nothing.

RETURN

Because I couldn't stop reading Rilke. Not really
reading but repeating the same lines
to myself over and over. Like masturbation.
Like one who's just discovered masturbation.
Like one who is compulsive
but tries to remember the freshness of discovery.
Fresh as a new rot blooming.
Because I was full of scandent pangs, livid wisteria.
And at every familiar street corner, for that matter, bursts
of small flowers rose up me like reflux.
My cross street. My for-the-time-being and
for-the-time-having-been. My undue nostalgia, sour
in an empty mouth. Because I didn't have much
to contribute to the conversation, I watched the lurid sky
over the bay with its tight jaw unhinged, as the butter-blond light
poured out. To this and that I pointed and said, Look,
it's beautiful. Don't take my word for it. Because, returning
to Reuterstraße years later, I missed someone. No,
I missed myself in certain time and location.
I saw what I had missed and I was never coming back.
I pressed my forehead against the closed wooden door.
Left a strange moisture there. Icky balm of having wanted.

HEIRLOOM

In the field, as a child, I slept on his chest,
small and fleshy like an extra lung.
The house smelled like smoke
but we were not alarmed.

Before he could move the cherry
of his cigarette, I ran into my father's arms.
Every reception like a bee sting.

My mother said the softest things
get torn into. And how soft and rotten I was
beside her smoldering, invulnerable silhouette.
I learned how to smoke behind the library

in winter. Get bitten, bite back.
In my grandmother's yard, I found a robin's egg.
I didn't know what I looked like yet.

The egg in my hand was speckled
and smooth. I thought, to keep it safe
I'll have to hold it, bury it.
You know how that goes.

Once I buried a stone in the sand
and the next day found in its place
a full-grown tomato plant. To receive

the world, sometimes you have to displace
expectation. The tomato was my father's prank,
but the pride was mine, as I offered him
wholeheartedly, the muscular fruit.

LILAC ODE

Like a giddy child,
like my cousin, who,
when we were young
would wake me several times
before dawn and ask,
Is it morning yet?
Will you look out
the window to check
if it's morning yet?,
you rose early.
You were alert
like that. Your very
odor, a gesture.
Your corolla,
a bundle of silk
arms opening,
the whole
inflorescence
reaching and waving.
Of the four staples
of summer, the others
being rain, skunk,
and cow shit,
you were first to leave.
You would not be held
onto. Some of your
little white hands

had already wilted
when Patty picked
me a bouquet
from my father's
yard, while he
and I sat for an hour,
talking till he was nearly
out of breath,
his eyes squinting
into the sun or wincing
in little jolts
of pain, but always
tightened, never
fully opened,
like a few
of your finicky buds.
Those sticky little
buds, alveoli,
a scented lung
that gives away
slowly at first,
till the blooms
slouch, breathless.

THE DRIVE

In the backseat, pressed
between J and F like a spent lilac
in a dictionary, I was unlasting.

There were lovebirds in the front
fricativing each other but it made
a which-way when C off-roaded

from an accidental exit. We belly-laughed.
My problem is always the saying
and sometimes the being overly heard.

Sometimes the under. God bless you.
But anyway, what better time to slip out
of your corset and let it settle

over your jeans? Gut-busted buttons,
we were laughing all the way to the capitol,
I tell you. That's what I said, isn't it? Anyway,

we read a lick of the monologues, stopped
for snacks at the Clara Barton service station
off the Jersey Turnpike, and played this game

where two players try to say the same
word simultaneously, but it's hard
to seem samely when you're having a good time

with all those in-betweens. Inside *tavern*
and *dowel*, a trickling. I felt a flutter
when we passed through Baltimore

but I didn't say it because what's the use?
I am overheard anyway and always elsewhering,
but no, not now. I will commit myself to the middle

seat and the press between
my breeze-ripened companions, who love
like berries farther down the bush.

PEOPLE FALL ALL THE TIME

On the farm there was a low music
to it. The goats bleated, the cows
bawled and bellowed and below
were the flats where the flames caught
the neighbor boy's Carhartts
and he learned every note; he howled

and lowed. Accident happens casually.
A branch breaks and the body lands
the wrong way. Snapping is easy.
Find the beat. The body is what it was
to be. Dad said Hay is for horses. Dad
said Hey Kiddo. Dad said Whoa now.
He didn't buy a phone so he could lay

low. He said Manual labor. He said The fall
as something you can take. He suffered
a break in a lonely way. Lo hello high hay,
the words in the marrow, the sow and the mare, Oh—
what stays are the song and the crash
of the tractor, the trash compactor, the machines
full of love and the fields full of breaking,
the fields where the light slips out.

ACKNOWLEDGMENTS

Thank you to the editors of the following journals, in which some of the poems in this collection were first published:

The Bennington Review: "A Series of Losses" and "In the Nets"
BOAAT: "Travel Narrative," "Slumber Party," and "On Taste"
Cosmonauts Avenue: "Something Important Put Clumsily Away"
Foundry: "Geosmin"
Jellyfish Magazine: "Practice Test for Insatiable Loneliness"
Memorious: "Syrinx"
Meridian: "Dredge"
Narrative Magazine: "Spring Cleaning," "Field Music," "Contrition," "My Love," "People Fall All the Time," and "Sonnet with a Line from Wordsworth"
Prelude: "Return"
Pouch: "I Contain Myself Needfully"
Tinderbox Poetry: "On Music" and "Proximity"
The Yale Review: "Appetite"
Zone 3: "Heirloom" and "Walking in Reverse"

I would like to extend my gratitude to all the people who supported me along each step of the way to realizing this book. Thanks to Rosanna Warren for believing in my manuscript, the staff and board members of the National Poetry Series for providing this opportunity, and Daniel Halpern, Gabriella Doob, and the rest of the team at Ecco Books for seeing it through with such care.

I am grateful to the New York University Creative Writing program, the NYU Graduate School of Arts and Sciences Provost's Global Research Initiative, and the Beinecke Foundation for their financial and academic support, which gave me the time, space, and guidance I needed to complete this project. Thanks to CC Perry and Hestia Artists' Residency. Thanks to the publishers mentioned above and to Benjamin Aleshire and *The Salon*. And thanks to the readers and editors who supported this manuscript on its way to finding a home.

I'd like to thank my teachers for challenging, supporting, and inspiring me: Major Jackson, Catherine Barnett, Yusef Komunyakaa, Sharon Olds, Brenda Shaughnessy, Rowan Ricardo Phillips, Ed Hirsch, Meghan O'Rourke, and Anne Carson and Bob Currie. Studying with Major at the University of Vermont inspired the beginnings of this manuscript, and Catherine's guidance during my time at NYU was crucial in continuing it. Thanks also to Dan Fogel, Eric Lindstrom, Huck Gutman, and Dennis Mahoney at UVM. Warmth and gratitude to my earlier teachers, who encouraged me to pursue my love of writing: Matt Schlein, Kathleen Distasio Brinegar, and Ann Brown.

To my beloved friends, readers, and workshop peers, thanks: Ama Codjoe, Maddie Mori, Jessie Modi, Sophia Holtz, Chase Berggrun, M'Bilia Meekers, Aria Aber, Holly Mitchell, Diannely Antigua, Rachel Mannheimer, Maggie Millner, Vanessa Moody, Lindsey Skillen, JJ Starr, Mallory Imler Powell, Yuxi Lin, Ian Spencer Bell, Zoe Goldstein, Adrian Coto, Alisa Koyrakh, Lizzie Delgado, Matthew Brailas, Jihyun Yun, Eleanor Wright, Momina Mela, Dacota Pratt-Pariseau, Henry Mills, Marco Yan, Yael Hacohen, and the rest of my cohort at NYU for sharing your friendship, your work, and your thoughtful suggestions.

So much love and thanks to Colin Dekeersgieter and Francisco Márquez. Your friendship gives me shape when I feel like I have none. Your poetry inspires me. I'm proud to be your friend.

And gratitude to the following friends for their inspiration and emotional, moral, and practical support: Ian Sherman, Maryse Smith, Joey Agresta, Padraic Reagan, Matt White, Meghan Polus, and Ashley Melander.

I can't thank my family enough, but I will keep trying.

And finally, thanks to Misha, for thinking, reading, and growing with me, and for being the person in my house.

NOTES

"Syrinx" quotes lines from "Ojos Azules," a song that has been attributed to several authors, including Gilberto Rojas Enríquez.

"On Looking" refers to Degas's *Young Woman with Ibis*.

"Filling Station" takes its first and last lines from Elizabeth Bishop's poem of the same name.

"Bloom" quotes a line from the 1934 song "Blue Moon," written by Richard Rodgers and Lorenz Hart.

"Sonnet with a Line from Wordsworth" takes the following line from William Wordsworth's *The Prelude*: "Bliss was it in that Dawn to be alive, / But to be young was very heaven!"

"Having Been" was written for a class with Ed Hirsch, as a very loose imitation of Czesław Miłosz's "Encounter."

"On Art" borrows bits of language from Rilke's *Letters to a Young Poet*, "Achy Breaky Heart," written by Don Von Tress and performed by Billy Ray Cyrus, Keats's "Ode on a Grecian Urn" and a letter from Keats to Benjamin Bailey, AC/DC's "You Shook Me All Night Long," and "Shake, Rattle and Roll" by Jesse Stone a.k.a. Charles E. Calhoun.

"My Mother the Astronomer" gives a little nod to Walt Whitman's "When I Heard the Learn'd Astronomer."

NATIONAL POETRY SERIES WINNERS

The National Poetry Series was established in 1978 to ensure the publication of five collections of poetry annually through five participating publishers. The Series is funded annually by Amazon Literary Partnership, the Gettinger Family Foundation, Bruce Gibney, HarperCollins Publishers, Stephen King, Lannan Foundation, Newman's Own Foundation, Anna and Olafur Olafsson, Penguin Random House, the Poetry Foundation, Elise and Steven Trulaske, and the National Poetry Series Board of Directors.

THE NATIONAL POETRY SERIES WINNERS OF 2019 OPEN COMPETITION

Field Music by Alexandria Hall
Chosen by Rosanna Warren for Ecco

Little Big Bully by Heid Erdrich
Chosen by Amy Gerstler for Penguin Books

Fractal Shores by Diane Louie
Chosen by Sherod Santos for University of Georgia Press

Thrown in the Throat by Benjamin Garcia
Chosen by Kazim Ali for Milkweed Editions

An Incomplete List of Names by Michael Torres
Chosen by Raquel Salas Rivera for Beacon Press